To Grandma,
for when you
wake up at night!
merry christmas! (1999)
Love Penny

Lewis Carroll's Bedside Book

LEWIS CARROLL'S
BEDSIDE BOOK

'entertainments for the wakeful hours'

Edited by Edgar Cuthwellis
with illustrations
by Lewis Carroll and Phuz

BOSTON
HOUGHTON MIFFLIN COMPANY
1979

Library of Congress Cataloging in Publication Data
Dodgson, Charles Lutwidge, 1832–1898.
Lewis Carroll's Bedside book.
I. Cuthwellis, Edgar.   I. Title.
PR4611.B4   1979   793.7′3   79–16708
ISBN 0–395–28596–8

Printed in the United States of America
P 10 9 8 7 6 5 4 3 2 1

With the exception of Mrs Beeton's 'nightcap recipes',
almost everything in this book was actually written by
Lewis Carroll. I have gathered the material together from
a wide variety of sources and in order to make it 'hang
together' as neatly as possible I have occasionally been
bold enough — fool enough, you may say — to add a few
linking words of my own in the manner of Lewis Carroll.
I hope that he — and you — will forgive my presumption.

The illustrations on pages 16 and 43–44 are by Lewis
Carroll. The remaining illustrations are by Phuz.

E.C.

❧ CONTENTS ❧

DO but consider what an excellent thing sleep is: it is so inestimable a jewel that, if a tyrant would give his crown for an hour's slumber, it cannot be bought: of so beautiful a shape is it, that though a man lie with an Empress, his heart cannot beat quite till he leaves her embracements to be at rest with the other: yea, so greatly indebted are we to this kinsman of death, that we owe the better tributary, half our life to him: and there is good cause why we should do so: for sleep is the golden chain that ties health and our bodies together. Who complains of want? of wounds? of cares? of great men's oppressions? of captivity? whilst he sleepeth? Beggars in their beds take as much pleasure as kings: can we therefore surfeit of this delicate ambrosia?

Thomas Dekker 1570–1632

❧ PILLOW PROBLEMS ❧

Calming Calculations

In preparing the second edition of my book *Pillow-Problems Thought Out During Sleepless Nights*, I replaced the words 'sleepless nights' by 'wakeful hours'. The change was made in order to allay the anxiety of kind friends, who had written to me to express their sympathy in my broken-down state of health, believing that I am a sufferer from chronic 'insomnia', and that it is as a remedy for that exhausting malady that I have recommended mathematical calculation.

The original title was not, I fear, wisely chosen; and it certainly *was* liable to suggest a meaning I did not intend to convey, viz. that my 'nights' are very often *wholly* 'sleepless'. This is by no means the case: I have never suffered from 'insomnia': and the over-wakeful hours, that I have had to spend at night, have often been simply the result of the over-sleepy hours I have spent during the preceding evening! Nor is it as a remedy for *wakefulness* that I have suggested mathematical calculation; but as a remedy for the *harassing thoughts* that are apt to invade a wholly-unoccupied mind.

To state the matter logically, the dilemma which my friends *suppose* me to be in has, for its two horns, the endurance of a sleepless night, and the adoption of some recipe for inducing sleep. Now, so far as *my* experience goes, no such recipe has any effect, unless when you are sleepy, and mathematical calculations would be more likely to delay, than to hasten, the advent of sleep.

The *real* dilemma, which I have had to face, is this: given that the brain is in so wakeful a condition that do what I will, I am *certain* to remain awake for the next hour or so, I must choose between two courses, viz. either to submit to the fruitless self-torture of going through some worrying topic, over and over again, or else to dictate to myself some topic sufficiently absorbing to keep the worry at bay. A mathematical problem *is*, for me, such a topic; and is a benefit, even if it lengthens the wakeful period a little. I believe that an hour of calculation is much better for me than half-an-hour of worry.

Even when it is a matter of the most elementary calculation, the process of arriving at a solution may involve a diverting dialogue, viz. the problem of 'The Two Clocks':

Which is better, a clock that is right only once a year, or a clock that is right twice every day?

'The latter,' you reply, 'unquestionably.' Very good, now attend.

I have two clocks: one doesn't go *at all*, and the other loses a minute a day: which would you prefer? 'The losing one', you answer, 'without a doubt.' Now observe: the one which loses a minute a day has to lose twelve hours, or seven hundred and twenty minutes before it is right again, consequently it is only right once in two years, whereas the other is evidently right as often as the time it points to comes round, which happens twice a day. You see that the clock is right *at* eight o'clock? Consequently, when eight o'clock comes round your clock is right.

'Yes, I see *that*,' you reply.

Very good, then you've contradicted yourself *twice*: now get out of the difficulty as best you can, and don't contradict yourself again if you can help it.

You *might* go on to ask, 'How am I to know when eight o'clock *does* come? My clock will not tell me.' Be patient: you know that when eight o'clock comes your clock is right, very good; then your rule is this: keep your eye fixed on your clock, and *the very moment it is right* it will be eight o'clock. 'But—,' you say. There, that'll do; the more you argue the farther you get from the point, so it will be as well to stop.

Here are ten calculations for you to attempt while lying awake at night. The first three are problems, the remainder mere puzzles. The solutions will be found at the back of the book.

I THE PIGS
Place twenty-four pigs in four sties so that, as you go round and round, you may always find the number in each sty nearer to ten than the number in the last.

2 THE CHELSEA PENSIONERS
If 70 per cent have lost an eye, 75 per cent an ear, 80 per cent an arm, 85 per cent a leg: what percentage, *at least*, must have lost all four?

3 THE TWO OMNIBUSES
Omnibuses start from a certain point, both ways, every 15 minutes. A traveller, starting on foot along with one of them, meets one in $12\frac{1}{2}$ minutes: when will he be overtaken by one?

4   Dreaming of apples on a wall,
        And dreaming often, dear,
      I dreamed that, if I counted all,
        —How many would appear?

5   A stick I found that weighed two pound:
        I sawed it up one day
      In pieces eight of equal weight!
        How much did each piece weigh?
        (Everybody says 'a quarter of a pound',
           which is wrong.)

6   John gave his brother James a box:
      About it there were many locks.

      James woke and said it gave him pain;
      So gave it back to John again.

      The box was not with lid supplied,
      Yet caused two lids to open wide:

      And all these locks had never a key—
      What kind of a box, then, could it be?

7 What is most like a bee in May?
      'Well, let me think : perhaps—' you say.
  Bravo! You're guessing well today!

8   Three sisters at breakfast
           were feeding the cat,
      The first gave it sole
           —Puss was grateful for that:
      The next gave it salmon
           —which Puss thought a treat:

The third gave it herring
  —which Puss wouldn't eat.
  (Explain the conduct of the cat.)

9 Said the Moon to the Sun,
   'Is the daylight begun?'
  Said the Sun to the Moon,
   'Not a minute too soon.'

  'You're a Full Moon,' said he.
   She replied with a frown,
  'Well! I never *did* see
   So uncivil a clown!'
  (Query: Why was the moon so angry?)

10 When the King found that his money was nearly all
gone, and that he really *must* live more economi-
cally, he decided on sending away most of his Wise
Men. There were some hundreds of them – very
fine old men, and magnificently dressed in green
velvet gowns with gold buttons: if they *had* a fault,
it was that they always contradicted one another
when he asked for their advice – and they certainly
ate and drank enormously. So, on the whole, he
was rather glad to get rid of them. But there was an
old law, which he did not dare to disobey, which
said that there must always be

  'Seven blind of both eyes:
   Two blind of one eye:
  Four that see with both eyes:
   Nine that see with one eye.'
  (Query: How many did he keep?)

Magic Numbers

While lying awake in bed consider the curious properties of certain 'magic numbers':

What is remarkable about 12345679 is that you can multiply it by 9, or *any* of the first nine multiples of 9, and you will get an answer which simply consists of a repetition of the same digit. Furthermore, the digit will be the same as the number of 9s in the multiplier.

$$12345679 \times 9 = 111111111$$
$$12345679 \times 18 = 222222222$$
$$12345679 \times 27 = 333333333$$
$$12345679 \times 36 = 444444444$$
$$12345679 \times 45 = 555555555$$
$$12345679 \times 54 = 666666666$$
$$12345679 \times 63 = 777777777$$
$$12345679 \times 72 = 888888888$$
$$12345679 \times 81 = 999999999$$

Multiply 100001 by any five-digit number you like and you will get a ten-digit answer made up of the five digits repeated twice.

$$100001 \times 12345 = 1234512345$$
$$100001 \times 54321 = 5432154321$$
$$100001 \times 67890 = 6789067890$$
$$100001 \times 98765 = 9876598765$$
$$100001 \times 13579 = 1357913579$$
$$100001 \times 24680 = 2468024680$$
$$100001 \times 99999 = 9999999999$$
$$100001 \times 69696 = 6969669696$$
$$100001 \times 10001 = 1000110001$$

142857 is a most magical 'magic number':

$$142857 \times 2 = 285714$$
$$142857 \times 3 = 428751$$
$$142857 \times 4 = 571428$$
$$142857 \times 5 = 714285$$
$$142857 \times 6 = 857142$$

You will notice that in each case the answer to the sum consists of the same six digits as in the original number and, though starting with a different digit each time, they are in the same order.

What happens when you multiply it by 7?

$$142857 \times 7 = 999999$$

999999 is *not* the answer you expected, but having arrived at it, look where it takes you:

142857 multiplied by 7 equals 999999
AND 999999 divided by 9 equals 111111!

285714 multiplied by 7 equals 1999998
AND 1999998 divided by 9 equals 222222!

428571 multiplied by 7 equals 2999997
AND 2999997 divided by 9 equals 333333!

571428 multiplied by 7 equals 3999996
AND 3999996 divided by 9 equals 444444!

714285 multiplied by 7 equals 4999995
AND 4999995 divided by 9 equals 555555!

857142 multiplied by 7 equals 5999995
AND 5999995 divided by 9 equals 666666!

Tangrams

Tangram is the name given to a Chinese geometrical puzzle consisting of a square dissected into five triangles, a square, and a rhomboid, which can be combined so as to make an infinite variety of figures. Having constructed your own set of Tangrams, attempt to recreate the four following figures. The solutions will be found at the back of the book.

The March Hare

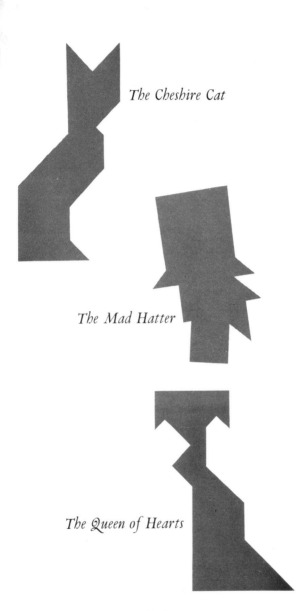

The Cheshire Cat

The Mad Hatter

The Queen of Hearts

The Labyrinth

Make your way from the inside of the labyrinth to the outside – or *vice versa*. You will find the correct path given at the back of the book.

Word Ways

1 A Russian had three sons. The first was named Rab and became a lawyer. The second was named Ymra and became a soldier. The third son became a sailor. What was his name?

2 Find a bird with the letters 'gp' as its nucleus.

3 Find a fruit with the letters 'emo' as its nucleus.

4 'Flit on, cheering angel.' Who is she?

5 'Wild agitator, means well.' Who is he?

The solutions can be found at the back of the book.

Doublets

Just a year ago last Christmas, two young ladies – smarting under that secret scourge of feminine humanity, the having 'nothing to do' – besought me to send them 'some riddles'. But riddles I had none at hand, and therefore set myself to devise some other form of verbal torture which should serve the same purpose. The result of my meditations was a new kind of Puzzle – new at least to me – which, now that it has been fairly tested by a year's experience and commended by many friends, I offer to you.

The rules of the Puzzle are simple enough. Two words are proposed, of the same length; and the puzzle consists in linking these together by interposing other words, each of which shall differ from the next word *in one letter only.* That is to say, one letter may be changed in one of the given words, then one letter in the word so obtained, and so on, till we arrive at the other given word. The letters must not be interchanged among themselves, but each must keep to his own place. As an example, the word 'head' may be changed into 'tail' by interposing the words 'heal, teal, tell, tall'. I call the two given words 'a Doublet', the interposed words 'links', and the entire series 'a Chain', of which I here append an example—

HEAD
h e a l
t e a l
t e l l
t a l l
TAIL

It is, perhaps, needless to state that it is *de rigueur* that the links should be English words, such as might be used in good society.

		Links needed
1	Make EEL into PIE	3
2	Turn POOR into RICH	5
3	Prove RAVEN to be MISER	3
4	Change OAT to RYE	3
5	Get WOOD from TREE	7
6	Prove GRASS to be GREEN	7
7	Evolve MAN from APE	5
8	Change CAIN into ABEL	8
9	Make FLOUR into BREAD	5
10	Make TEA HOT	3

The solutions can be found at the back of the book.

Board Game for One

Throw a dice and advance the number of squares indicated. In the event of landing on a square featuring a drawing of any kind, return to the very first square and begin again. Sleep is almost certain to have overwhelmed the player before he reaches the final square.

❧ NIGHT WRITING ❧

How best to keep warm in bed has long been a dilemma to me. How to write in bed has been a problem too, but it is one I have solved with a simple mechanical appliance that I have named the 'Nyctograph'. I invented it on September 24th 1891, but I do not intend to patent it. Anyone who chooses is welcome to make and sell the article.

Anyone who has tried, as I have often done, the process of getting out of bed at 2 a.m. in a winter night, lighting a candle, and recording some happy thought which would probably be otherwise forgotten, will agree with me it entails much discomfort. All I have now to do, if I wake and think of something I wish to record, is to draw from under the pillow a small memorandum book, containing my Nyctograph, write a few lines, or even a few pages, without even putting the hands outside the bed-clothes, replace the book, and go to sleep again.

There is an ingenious machine already made and sold (I bought mine from Messrs Elliot, 101 St Martin's Lane), where you write a line of MS inside a narrow oblong opening, then turn a handle till you hear a click; this shifts the paper upwards and gives a fresh surface for another line of MS.

I tried to put this into a more portable shape, by cutting a series of oblong apertures in a piece of pasteboard the size of a page of a small memorandum book; but the writing is apt to be illegible, as it is difficult to know where you are, and you constantly come against the edge of the aperture when you wish to go further in order to make the loop of an 'h' or the tail of a 'y'. Then I tried rows of square holes, each to hold one letter (quarter of an inch square I found a very convenient size), and this proved a much better plan than the former; but the letters were still apt to be illegible. Then I said to myself 'Why not invent a square alphabet, using only dots at the corners, and lines along the sides?' I soon found that, to make the writing easy to read, it was necessary to know where each square began. This I secured by the rule that *every* square-letter should contain a large black dot in the North West corner. Also I found that it would cause confusion to have any symbol which used only the West side of the square. These limitations reduced the number of available symbols to 31, of which I selected 26 for the letters of the alphabet, and succeeded in getting 23 of them to have a distinct resemblance to the letters they were to represent.

In the following list, I call the North East corner '2', the South West corner '3', and the South East corner '4'. Also I have bracketed letters whose symbols run in pairs, each being the reverse of the other. Every symbol is assumed to have a large dot in its North West corner.

	Corners	Sides	Resemblance to letters, etc.
A	4	none	right-hand side of 'A'
B	2, 4	W	vertical line of 'B', with dots to stand for the semi-circles.
C	none	N,W,S	obvious
D	none	N,E,S	obvious; also reverse of preceding symbol
E	none	N	top of 'E'; taken as simplest symbol for commonest letter
F	4	N,W	obvious; dot stands for cross-piece which has fallen off
G	2	W,S	analogous to symbol for 'C'; also reverse of preceding symbol
H	none	W,E	obvious
I	none	S	like 'i', vertical line having fallen down
J	none	E,S	like 'j', dot having slipped to one side
K	4	W	vertical line, and foot, of 'K'
L	none	W,S	obvious
M	none	N,W,E	like 'm', with central vertical erased
N	none	W,E,S	reverse of preceding symbol
O	none	N,W,E,S	obvious
P	2	W	vertical line of 'p', with dot to stand for the semicircle
Q	none	E	vertical line of 'q', with dot to stand for the semicircle; also reverse of preceding symbol
R	3	N,E	lower part of 'R'
S	none	N,W	like old-fashioned 's'
T	none	N,E	left-hand part of 'T'; also reverse of preceding symbol
U	2	none	tops of 'U'
V	2, 4	none	corners of 'V'
W	2	S	like 2 'V' symbols, with lower corners connected by a line
X	3	N	no likeness claimed
Y	4	N	ditto, but is reverse of preceding symbol
Z	none	N,S	upper and lower lines of 'Z'

	Corners	Sides	Meaning
'figures'	2, 3	none	corners of 'F'; means 'symbols will now represent figures'
'date'	2, 3, 4	none	corners of a square 'D'; means 'next 6 symbols will represent date, 2 standing for day of month, 2 for month, and 2 for year of century (e.g. '070305' would represent 7th March 1805)
'letters'	3, 4	none	corners of 'L'; means 'symbols will now represent letters again'
'and'	3	E	symbol for 'A' put upright; and right-hand portions of symbols for 'N' and 'D'
'the'	3, 4	N	upper portion of symbol for 'T'; feet of symbol for 'H'; and symbol for 'E'

When the symbols are to represent figures, they should be the symbols for 10 of the letters, as follows:

	Letters	Reasons for Selection
1	B	first consonant
2	D	initial of 'duo' and 'deux'
3	T	initial of 'three'
4	F	initial of 'four'
5	L	means '50'
6	S	initial of 'six'
7	M	finial of 'septem'
8	H	initial of 'huit'; also resembles '8'
9	N	initial of 'nine'
0	Z	initial of 'zero'

These 10 letters are a portion of my 'Memoria Technica', in which (by assigning 2 consonants to each digit, and assigning no meanings to vowels and 'Y') I can always represent any date, or other number, by a *real* word: the other 10 consonants being as follows: '1,C; 2,W; 3,J; 4,Q; 5,V; 6,X; 7,P; 8,K; 9,G; 0,R.' There are reasons for selection in all these pairs, except '3,J', which had to pair off as the sole survivors.

Rules for Letter Writing

Much of my correspondence is conducted late at night. Indeed it is not uncommon for me still to be writing letters at three o'clock in the morning. Whatever time *you* choose to conduct *your* correspondence, the art of letter-writing involves certain rules that should *never* be broken be it ever so late—or so early.

HOW TO BEGIN A LETTER

If the Letter is to be in answer to another, begin by getting out that other letter and reading it through, in order to refresh your memory, as to what it is you have to answer, and as to your correspondent's *present address* (otherwise you will be sending your letter to his regular address in *London*, though he has been careful in writing to give you his *Torquay* address in full).

Next, Address and Stamp the Envelope. 'What! Before writing the *Letter*?' Most certainly. And I'll tell you what will happen if you don't. You will go on writing till the last moment, and, just in the middle of the last sentence, you will become aware that 'time's up!' Then comes the hurried wind-up – the wildly-scrawled signature – the hastily-fastened envelope, which comes open in the post – the address, a mere hieroglyphic – the horrible discovery that you've forgotten to replenish your Stamp-case – the frantic appeal, to everyone in the house, to lend you a stamp – the headlong rush to the Post Office, arriving, hot and gasping, just after the box has closed – and finally, a week afterwards, the return of the Letter, from the Dead-Letter Office, marked 'address illegible'!

Next, put your own address, *in full*, at the top of the note-sheet. It is an aggravating thing—I speak from bitter experience—when a friend, staying at some new address, heads his letter 'Dover', simply, assuming that you can get the rest of the address from his previous letter, which perhaps you have destroyed.

Next, put the date *in full*. It is another aggravating thing, when you wish, years afterwards, to arrange a series of letters, to find them dated 'Feb.17', 'Aug. 2', without any *year* to guide you as to which comes first. And never, never, dear Madam (N.B. this remark is addressed to ladies *only*: no *man* would ever do such a thing), put 'Wednesday', simply, as the date!

'That way madness lies.'

HOW TO GO ON WITH A LETTER

Here is a golden Rule to begin with. *Write legibly.* The average temper of the human race would be perceptibly sweetened, if everybody obeyed this Rule! A great deal of the bad writing in the world comes simply from writing *too quickly*. Of course you reply, 'I do it to save *time*.' A very good object, no doubt: but what right have you to do it at your friend's expense? Isn't *his* time as valuable as yours? Years ago, I used to receive letters from a friend — and very interesting letters too — written in one of the most atrocious hands ever invented. It generally took me about a *week* to read one of his letters. I used to carry it about in my pocket, and take it out at leisure times, to puzzle over the riddles which composed it — holding it in different positions and at different distances, till at last the meaning of some hopeless scrawl would flash upon me, when I at once wrote down the English under it; and, when several had been thus guessed, the context would help with the others, till at last the whole series of hieroglyphics was deciphered. If *all* one's friends wrote like that, Life would be entirely spent in reading their letters!

My second Rule is, don't fill *more* than a page and a half with apologies for not having written sooner!

The best subject, to *begin* with, is your friend's last letter. Write with the letter open before you. Answer his questions, and make any remarks his letter suggests. *Then* go on to what you want to say yourself. This arrangement is more courteous, and pleasanter for the reader, than to fill the letter with your own invaluable remarks, and then hastily answer your friend's questions in a postscript. Your friend is much more likely to enjoy your wit, *after* his own anxiety for information has been satisfied.

A few more Rules may fitly be given here, for correspondence that has unfortunately become *controversial*.

One is, *don't repeat yourself*. When once you have said your say, fully and clearly, on a certain point, and have failed to convince your friend, *drop that subject*: to repeat your arguments, all over again, will simply lead to his doing the same.

Another Rule is, when you have written a letter that you feel may possibly irritate your friend, however necessary you may have felt it to so express yourself, *put it aside till the next day*. Then read it over again, and fancy it addressed to yourself. This will often lead to your writing it all over again, taking out a lot of the vinegar and pepper, and putting in honey instead, and thus making a *much* more palatable dish of it! If, when you have done your best to write inoffensively, you still feel that it will probably lead to further controversy, *keep a copy of it*. There is very little use, months afterwards, in pleading 'I am almost sure I never expressed myself as you say: to the best of my recollection I said so-and-so'. *Far* better to be able to write: 'I did *not* express myself so: these are the words I used.'

My fifth Rule is, if your friend makes a severe remark, either leave it unnoticed, or make your reply distinctly *less* severe: and if he makes a friendly remark, tending towards 'making-up' the little difference that has arisen between you, let your reply be distinctly *more* friendly. If, in picking a quarrel, each party declined to go more than three-eighths of the way, and if, in making friends, each was ready to go five-eighths of the way – why, there would be more reconciliations than quarrels! Which is like the Irishman's remonstrance to his gad-about daughter—'Shure, you're *always* goin' out! You go out *three* times, for *wanst* that you come in!'

My sixth Rule (and my last remark about controversial correspondence) is, *don't try to have the last word!* How many a controversy would be nipped in the bud, if each was anxious to let the *other* have the last word! Never mind how telling a rejoinder you leave unuttered: never mind your friend's supposing that you are silent from lack of anything to say: let the thing drop, as soon as it is possible without discourtesy: remember 'speech is silvern, but silence is golden'! (N.B.—If you are a gentleman, and your friend is a lady, this Rule is superfluous: *you won't get the last word!*)

My seventh Rule is, if it should ever occur to you to write, jestingly, in *dispraise* of your friend, be sure you exaggerate enough to make the jesting *obvious*: a word spoken in *jest*, but taken as earnest, may lead to very serious consequences.

My eighth Rule. When you say, in your letter, 'I enclose cheque for £5,' or 'I enclose John's letter for you to see', leave off writing for a moment – go and get the document referred to – and *put it into the envelope*. Otherwise, you are pretty certain to find it lying about, after the post has gone!

My ninth Rule. When you get to the end of a notesheet, and find you have more to say, take another piece of paper – a whole sheet, or a scrap, as the case may demand: but whatever you do, *don't cross!* Remember the old proverb *'Cross-writing makes cross reading'*. 'The *old* proverb?' you say, inquiringly, *'How* old?' Well, not so *very* ancient, I must confess. In fact, I'm afraid I invented it while writing this paragraph! Still, you know, 'old' is a *comparative* term. I think you would be *quite* justified in addressing a chicken, just out of the shell, as 'Old boy!' *when compared* with another chicken, that was only half-out!

HOW TO END A LETTER

If doubtful whether to end with 'yours faithfully', or 'yours truly', or 'yours most truly', &c. (there are at least a dozen varieties, before you reach 'yours affectionately'), refer to your correspondent's last letter, and make your winding-up *at least as friendly as his*: in fact, even if a shade *more* friendly, it will do no harm!

A Postscript is a very useful invention: but it is *not* meant (as so many ladies suppose) to contain the real *gist* of the letter: it serves rather to throw into the shade any little matter we do *not* wish to make a fuss about. For example, you friend had promised to execute a commission for you in town, but forgot it, thereby putting you to great inconvenience: and he now writes to apologise for his negligence. It would be cruel, and needlessly crushing, to make it the main subject of your reply. How much more gracefully it comes in thus: 'P.S. Don't distress yourself any more about having omitted that little matter in town. I won't deny that it *did* put my plans out a little, at the time, but it's all right now. I often forget things myself: and "those who live in glasshouses mustn't throw stones", you know!'

When you take your letters to the Post, *carry them in your hand*. If you put them in your pocket you will take a long country-walk (I speak from experience), passing the Post-Office *twice*, going and returning, and, when you get home, you will find them *still* in your pocket.

Letter to a Child-Friend

Lately I have been awfully busy, and I've had to write *heaps* of letters – wheelbarrows full, almost. And it tires me so that generally I go to bed again the next minute after I get up: and sometimes I go to bed again a minute *before* I get up! Did you ever hear of any one being so tired as *that*? . . .

The letters I enjoy writing most of all are the ones I send to the child-friends who have brightened my life. Usually the child becomes so entirely a different being as she grows into a woman, that our friendship has to change too: and *that* it usually does by gliding down from a loving intimacy into an acquaintance that merely consists of a smile and a bow when we meet!

But while my child-friends remain *children* I can write them as I please, viz:

Christ Church,
Oxford
December 15, 1875.

My dear Magdalen,—I want to explain to you why I did not call yesterday. I was sorry to miss you, but you see I had so many conversations on the way. I tried to explain to the people in the street that I was going to see you, but they wouldn't listen; they said they were in a hurry, which was rude. At last I met a wheelbarrow that I thought would attend to me, but I couldn't make out what was in it. I saw some features at first, then I looked through a telescope, and found it was a countenance; then I looked through a microscope, and found it was a face! I thought it was rather like me, so I fetched a large looking-glass to make sure, and then to my great joy I found it was me. We shook hands, and were just beginning to talk, when myself came up and joined us, and we had quite a pleasant conversation. I said, 'Do you remember when we all met at Sandown?' and myself said, 'It was very jolly there; there was a child called Magdalen,' and me said, 'I used to like her a little; not much you know – only a little.' Then it was time for us to go to the train, and who do you think came to the station to see us off? You would never guess, so I must tell you. They were two very dear friends of mine, who happen to be here just now, and beg to be allowed to sign this letter as your affectionate friends,

Lewis Carroll and C. L. Dodgson.

The Alphabet Cipher

In order to write in the dark you may make use of my Nyctograph. In order to keep others 'in the dark' as to what you are writing, you should use the Alphabet Cipher.

Each column of this table forms a dictionary of symbols representing the alphabet: thus, in the A column, the symbol is the same as the letter represented; in the B column, A is represented by B, B by C, and so on.

To use the table, some word or sentence should be agreed on by two correspondents. This may be called the 'key-word', or 'key-sentence', and should be carried in the memory only.

In sending a message, write the key-word over it, letter for letter, repeating it as often as may be necessary: the letters of the key-word will indicate which column is to be used in translating each letter of the message, the symbols for which should be written underneath: then copy out the symbols only, and destroy the first paper. It will now be impossible for anyone, ignorant of the keyword, to decipher the message, even with the help of the table.

For example, let the key-word be *vigilance*, and the message 'meet me on Tuesday evening at seven', the first paper will read as follows—

```
v i gi l ancevi gi l ancevi gi l ancevi
m e e t meontue s dayeveni ngat seven
h mkbx ebpxpmyl l yrxi i qt ol tf gzzv
```

The second will contain only 'hmkbxebpxpmyllyrx- iiqtoltfgzzv'.

The receiver of the message can, by the same process, retranslate it into English.

	A	B	C	D	E	F	G	H	I	J	K	L	M	N	O	P	Q	R	S	T	U	V	W	X	Y	Z	
A	a	b	c	d	e	f	g	h	i	j	k	l	m	n	o	p	q	r	s	t	u	v	w	x	y	z	A
B	b	c	d	e	f	g	h	i	j	k	l	m	n	o	p	q	r	s	t	u	v	w	x	y	z	a	B
C	c	d	e	f	g	h	i	j	k	l	m	n	o	p	q	r	s	t	u	v	w	x	y	z	a	b	C
D	d	e	f	g	h	i	j	k	l	m	n	o	p	q	r	s	t	u	v	w	x	y	z	a	b	c	D
E	e	f	g	h	i	j	k	l	m	n	o	p	q	r	s	t	u	v	w	x	y	z	a	b	c	d	E
F	f	g	h	i	j	k	l	m	n	o	p	q	r	s	t	u	v	w	x	y	z	a	b	c	d	e	F
G	g	h	i	j	k	l	m	n	o	p	q	r	s	t	u	v	w	x	y	z	a	b	c	d	e	f	G
H	h	i	j	k	l	m	n	o	p	q	r	s	t	u	v	w	x	y	z	a	b	c	d	e	f	g	H
I	i	j	k	l	m	n	o	p	q	r	s	t	u	v	w	x	y	z	a	b	c	d	e	f	g	h	I
J	j	k	l	m	n	o	p	q	r	s	t	u	v	w	x	y	z	a	b	c	d	e	f	g	h	i	J
K	k	l	m	n	o	p	q	r	s	t	u	v	w	x	y	z	a	b	c	d	e	f	g	h	i	j	K
L	l	m	n	o	p	q	r	s	t	u	v	w	x	y	z	a	b	c	d	e	f	g	h	i	j	k	L
M	m	n	o	p	q	r	s	t	u	v	w	x	y	z	a	b	c	d	e	f	g	h	i	j	k	l	M
N	n	o	p	q	r	s	t	u	v	w	x	y	z	a	b	c	d	e	f	g	h	i	j	k	l	m	N
O	o	p	q	r	s	t	u	v	w	x	y	z	a	b	c	d	e	f	g	h	i	j	k	l	m	n	O
P	p	q	r	s	t	u	v	w	x	y	z	a	b	c	d	e	f	g	h	i	j	k	l	m	n	o	P
Q	q	r	s	t	u	v	w	x	y	z	a	b	c	d	e	f	g	h	i	j	k	l	m	n	o	p	Q
R	r	s	t	u	v	w	x	y	z	a	b	c	d	e	f	g	h	i	j	k	l	m	n	o	p	q	R
S	s	t	u	v	w	x	y	z	a	b	c	d	e	f	g	h	i	j	k	l	m	n	o	p	q	r	S
T	t	u	v	w	x	y	z	a	b	c	d	e	f	g	h	i	j	k	l	m	n	o	p	q	r	s	T
U	u	v	w	x	y	z	a	b	c	d	e	f	g	h	i	j	k	l	m	n	o	p	q	r	s	t	U
V	v	w	x	y	z	a	b	c	d	e	f	g	h	i	j	k	l	m	n	o	p	q	r	s	t	u	V
W	w	x	y	z	a	b	c	d	e	f	g	h	i	j	k	l	m	n	o	p	q	r	s	t	u	v	W
X	x	y	z	a	b	c	d	e	f	g	h	i	j	k	l	m	n	o	p	q	r	s	t	u	v	w	X
Y	y	z	a	b	c	d	e	f	g	h	i	j	k	l	m	n	o	p	q	r	s	t	u	v	w	x	Y
Z	z	a	b	c	d	e	f	g	h	i	j	k	l	m	n	o	p	q	r	s	t	u	v	w	x	y	Z

My Fairy

I have a fairy by my side
   Which says I must not sleep,
When once in pain I loudly cried
   It said 'You must not weep'.

If, full of mirth, I smile and grin,
   It says 'You must not laugh',
When once I wished to drink some gin
   It said 'You must not quaff'.

When once a meal I wished to taste
   It said 'You must not bite';
When to the wars I went in haste
   It said 'You must not fight'.

'What may I do?' at length I cried,
   Tired of the painful task.
The fairy quietly replied,
   And said 'You must not ask'.

Moral: 'You mustn't.'

Again and again I have said to myself, on lying down at night, after a day embittered by some vexatious matter, 'I will *not* think of it any more! I have gone through it all, thoroughly. It can do no good whatever to go through it again. I *will* think of something else!' And in another ten minutes I have found myself, once more, in the very thick of the miserable business, and torturing myself, to no purpose, with all the old troubles.

Now it is not possible – this, I think, all psychologists will admit – by any effort of volition, to carry out the resolution 'I will *not* think of so-and-so.' (Witness the common trick, played on a child, of saying 'I'll give you a penny if you'll stand in that corner for five minutes, and *not once* think of strawberry-jam.' No human child ever yet won the tempting wager!) But it *is* possible – as I am most thankful to know – to carry out the resolution 'I *will* think of so-and-so.' Once fasten the attention upon a subject so chosen, and you will find that the worrying subject, which you desire to banish, is *practically* annulled. It may recur, from time to time – just looking in at the door, so to speak; but it will find itself so coldly received, and will get so little attention paid to it, that it will, after a while, cease to be any worry at all.

Perhaps I may venture, for a moment, to use a more serious tone, and to point out that there are mental troubles, much worse than mere worry, for which an absorbing subject of thought may serve as a remedy. There are sceptical thoughts, which seem for the moment to uproot the firmest faith; there are blasphemous thoughts, which dart unbidden into the most reverent souls; there are unholy thoughts, which torture, with their hateful presence, the fancy that would fain be pure.

Verses with a Moral

Composing original verses in one's head while lying in bed is mental *work* that *relaxes* one. Should the verses have a moral they may even *uplift* one at the same time.

BROTHER AND SISTER

'Sister, sister, go to bed!
Go and rest your weary head.'
Thus the prudent brother said.

'Do you want a battered hide,
Or scratches to your face applied?'
Thus his sister calm replied.

'Sister, do not raise my wrath.
I'd make you into mutton broth
As easily as kill a moth!'

The sister raised her beaming eye
And looked on him indignantly
And sternly answered, 'Only try!'

Off to the cook he quickly ran,
'Dear Cook, please lend a frying-pan
To me as quickly as you can.'

'And wherefore should I lend it you?'
'The reason, Cook, is plain to view.
I wish to make an Irish stew.'

'What meat is in that stew to go?'
'My sister'll be the contents!'
                                    'Oh!'
'You'll lend the pan to me, Cook?'
                                    'No!'

Moral: Never stew your sister.

PUNCTUALITY

Man naturally loves delay,
    And to procrastinate:
Business put off from day to day
    Is always done too late.

Let every hour be in its place
    Firm fixed, nor loosely shift,
And well enjoy the vacant space,
    As though a birthday gift.

And when the hour arrives, be *there*,
    Where'er that 'there' may be;
Uncleanly hands or ruffled hair
    Let no one ever see.

If dinner at 'half-past' be placed,
    At 'half-past then be dressed.
If at a 'quarter-past' make haste
    To be down with the rest.

Better to be before your time,
  Than e'er to be behind;
To ope the door while strikes the chime,
  That shows a punctual mind.

Moral

Let punctuality and care
  Seize every flitting hour,
So shalt thou cull a floweret fair,
  E'en from a fading flower.

Dilutions

Why is it that Poetry has never yet been subjected to
that process of Dilution which has proved so advan-
tageous to her sister-art Music? The Diluter gives us
first a few notes of some well-known air, then a dozen
bars of his own, then a few more notes of the air, and so
on alternately; thus saving the listener, if not from all
risk of recognising the melody at all, at least from the
too-exciting transports which it might produce in a
more concentrated form. The process is termed 'setting' by Composers, and any one that has ever ex-
perienced the emotion of being unexpectedly set down
in a heap of mortar, will recognise the truthfulness of
this happy phrase.

For truly, just as the genuine Epicure lingers lov-
ingly over a morsel of supreme Venison – whose every
fibre seems to murmur 'Excelsior!' – yet swallows, ere
returning to the toothsome dainty, great mouthfuls
of oatmeal-porridge and winkles: and just as the perfect
Connoisseur in Claret permits him but one delicate sip,

and then tosses off a pint or more of boarding-school beer: so also—

> I never loved a dear Gazelle—
>> *Nor anything that cost me much:*
> *High prices profit those who sell,*
>> *But why should I be fond of such?*

> To glad me with his soft black eye
>> *My son comes trotting home from school;*
> *He's had a fight but can't tell why—*
>> *He always was a little fool!*

> But, when he came to know me well,
>> *He kicked me out, her testy Sire:*
> *And when I stained my hair, that Belle*
>> *Might note the change, and thus admire*

> And love me, it was sure to dye
>> *A muddy green, or staring blue:*
> *Whilst one might trace, with half an eye,*
>> *The still triumphant carrot through.*

The first line of each verse is taken from a quatrain in Thomas Moore's poem *The Fire Worshippers*. I 'diluted' Moore by adding the lines in italic. As a diversion during a sleepless night, choose a favourite verse by one of the great poets and 'dilute' it with some additional lines of your own.

If Dilution is impossible – alas, you can remember *none* of the verses of the great poets! – you will have no alternative but to compose original Acrostics, Charades and Limericks.

Acrostic

This acrostic was composed for a favourite child-friend, Agnes Georgina Hull.

Around my lonely hearth tonight,
    Ghostlike the shadows wander:
Now here, now there, a childish sprite,
Earthborn and yet as angel bright,
    Seems near me as I ponder.

Gaily she shouts: the laughing air
    Echoes her note of gladness—
Or bends herself with earnest care
Round fairy-fortress to prepare
Grim battlement or turret-stair—
    In childhood's merry madness!

New raptures still hath youth in store.
    Age may but fondly cherish
Half-faded memories of yore—
Up, craven heart! repine no more!
Love stretches hands from shore to shore:
    Love is, and shall not perish!

Charade

One may combine a puzzle with a poem and create a versified riddle, like this Charade:

A CHARADE.

[NB FIVE POUNDS will be
given to any one who succeeds in
writing an original poetical Cha-
-rade, introducing the line "My
First is followed by a bird," but
making no use of the answer to
this Charade   Ap 8 1878
          (signed)
               Lewis Carroll]

My First is singular at best
      More plural is my Second
My Third is far the pluralest —
So plural-plural, I protest,
      It scarcely can be reckoned!

My First is followed by a bir
      My Second by believers
In magic art · my simple Thir
Follows, too often, hopes absurd,
      And plausible deceivers

My First to get at wisdom tries —
      A failure melancholy!
My Second men revere as wise ·
My Third from heights of wisdom fl
      To depths of frantic folly!

My First is ageing day by day,
  My Second's age is ended
My Third enjoys an age, they say,
That never seems to fade away,
  Through centuries extended!

My Whole? I need a Poet's pen
  To paint her myriad phases
The monarch, and the slave, of men —
A mountain-summit, and a den
  Of dark and deadly mazes!

A flashing light — a fleeting shade —
  Beginning, end, and middle
Of all that human art hath made,
Or wit devised! Go, seek her aid,
  If you would guess my riddle!

The solution to the Charade can be found at the back of the book.

Limericks

There was a young lady of station,
'I love man' was her sole exclamation:
    But when men cried, 'You flatter,'
    She replied, 'Oh! no matter,
Isle of Man is the true explanation.'

There was an old farmer of Readall,
Who made holes in his face with a needle,
    Then went *far* deeper in
    Than to pierce through the skin,
And yet strange to say he was made beadle.

There was an eccentric old draper,
Who wore a hat made of brown paper,
    It went up to a point,
    Yet it looked out of joint,
The cause of which *he* said was 'vapour'.

There was once a young man of Oporta,
Who daily got shorter and shorter,
    The reason he said
    Was the hod on his head,
Which was filled with the *heaviest* mortar.

His sister, named Lucy O'Finner,
Grew constantly thinner and thinner;
    The reason was plain,
    She slept out in the rain,
And was never allowed any dinner.

❧ GHOSTS AND NIGHTCAPS ❧

Phantasmagoria

One winter night, at half-past nine,
    Cold, tired, and cross, and muddy,
I had come home, too late to dine,
And supper, with cigars and wine,
    Was waiting in the study.

There was a strangeness in the room,
    And Something white and wavy
Was standing near me in the gloom—
I took it for the carpet-broom
    Left by that careless slavey.

But presently the Thing began
    To shiver and to sneeze:
On which I said 'Come, come, my man!
That's a most inconsiderate plan,
    Less noise there, if you please!'

'I've caught a cold', the Thing replies,
    'Out there upon the landing.'
I turned to look in some surprise,
And there, before my very eyes,
    A Little Ghost was standing!

When encountering a ghost for the first time it is
necessary to remain as calm as may be and to retain the
normal courtesies of civilized society, viz. on meeting a
ghost in the street after dark a gentleman should *always*

raise his hat. However should you be lying in bed affeared lest you might meet a ghost, having never met one before, the simplest method of allaying those fears is to conjure up a shadowy ghost of your own.

Shadow Play

> I dreamt I dwelt in marble halls,
> And each damp thing that creeps and crawls
> Went wobble-wobble on the walls.

By positioning your hands so as to form certain configurations and by placing your hands between a source of light — be it a moonbeam or a lamp — and a blank wall, you can ensure that what goes wobble-wobble on your bedroom wall is not a fiend but a friend.

The White Rabbit

The Cheshire Cat

The Carpenter

The March Hare

A Goat

A Camel

A Swan

A Wolf

Eat Wisely

Methought I walked a dismal place
    Dim horrors all around;
The air was thick with many a face,
    And black as night the ground.

I saw a monster come with speed,
    Its face of grimmliest green,
On human beings used to feed,
    Most dreadful to be seen.

I could not speak, I could not fly,
    I fell down in that place,
I saw the monster's horrid eye
    Come leering in my face!

Amidst my scarcely-stifled groans,
    Amidst my moanings deep,
I heard a voice, 'Wake! Mr Jones,
    You're screaming in your sleep!'

Restless nights and dreams that frighten and alarm us are all too frequently the result of an unfortunate evening meal. In a desultory conversation on a point connected with the dinner at our high table, the Senior Censor incidentally remarked to me that lobster-sauce, 'though a necessary adjunct to turbot, was not entirely wholesome'. It is entirely unwholesome. I never ask for it without reluctance. I never take a second spoonful without a feeling of apprehension on the subject of possible nightmare.

Eat Well

If peace of mind and a restful night are wanted, what one chooses to eat at the dinner table is a matter of considerable moment. How one chooses to *behave* at the dinner table is of no less significance. Indeed, in the hope of being of some assistance to those diners-out who are unacquainted with the usages of society I append a few 'hints for etiquette' that I trust may be of some small value:

In proceeding to the dining-room, the gentleman gives one arm to the lady he escorts – it is unusual to offer both.

The practice of taking soup with the next gentleman but one is now wisely discontinued; but the custom of asking your host his opinion of the weather immediately on the removal of the first course still prevails.

To use a fork with your soup, intimating at the same time to your hostess that you are reserving the spoon for the beefsteaks, is a practice wholly exploded.

On meat being placed before you, there is no possible objection to your eating it, if so disposed; still, in all such delicate cases, be guided entirely by the conduct of those around you.

It is always allowable to ask for artichoke jelly with your boiled venison; however, there are houses where this is not supplied.

The method of helping roast turkey with two carving-forks is practicable, but deficient in grace.

We do not recommend the practice of eating cheese with a knife and fork in one hand, and a spoon and wineglass in the other; there is a kind of awkwardness in the action which no amount of practice can entirely dispel.

As a general rule, do not kick the shins of the opposite gentleman under the table, if personally unacquainted with him; your pleasantry is liable to be misunderstood – a circumstance at all times unpleasant.

Proposing the health of the boy in buttons immediately on the removal of the cloth is a custom springing from regard to his tender years, rather than from a strict adherence to the rules of etiquette.

Nightcaps

How one behaves and what one eats at the dinner-table are matters of consequence. What one drinks at dinner is a matter of importance as well. When they are dining at my table I offer my guests a variety of drinks. My lady-guests mostly prefer draught-lemonade—but they can have any of the following beverages: (1) bottled lemonade; (2) ginger-beer; (3) beer; (4) water; (5) milk; (6) vinegar; (7) ink. Nobody has yet chosen either No. 6 or No. 7 . . .

In the matter of 'nightcaps' I am indebted to Mrs Samuel Beeton for the following suggestions. The first three beverages are *entirely* soothing. The remaining three may be considered more *stimulating*.

COCOA

Ingredients: Allow 2 teaspoonfuls of the prepared cocoa, or one of Cadbury's Cocoa Essence, to 1 breakfast-cup of boiling milk and boiling water.

Mode: Put the cocoa into a breakfast-cup, pour over it sufficient cold milk to make it into a smooth paste; then add equal quantities of boiling milk and boiling water, and stir all well together. Care must be taken not to allow the milk to get burnt, as it will entirely spoil the flavour of the preparation. The rock cocoa, or that bought in a solid piece, should be scraped, and made in the same manner, taking care to rub down all the lumps before the boiling liquid is added. All cocoa is better boiled for a minute or two.

Sufficient: 2 teaspoonfuls of prepared cocoa, or 1 of Cadbury's Cocoa Essence, for 1 breakfast-cup, or $\frac{1}{4}$ oz. of the rock cocoa for the same quantity.

MILK DRINK

Ingredients: 1 pint of new milk, 1 pint of water, salt to taste, 1 egg.

Mode: Pour the milk and water together, beat up the egg with the salt, and add it, mixing thoroughly.

Time: 2 minutes. Average Cost, 3d.

Sufficient to make 1 quart.

BEEF-TEA *(Baron Liebig's Method)*

Mode: Mince very finely $\frac{1}{2}$ lb of lean beef, put it in a glass or cup (not in metal) and pour on it $\frac{3}{4}$ pint of cold water, 4 drops of muriatic acid, and half a saltspoonful of salt. Let it stand for an hour, then strain it through a hair sieve, and rinse the residue with another $\frac{1}{4}$ pint of water.

This is quite transparent, and contains the albumen in solution. It should be taken cold, or, if heated, it should not be above 120°Fahr.

EGG WINE

Ingredients: 1 egg, 2 tablespoonfuls of cold water, 1 glass of sherry, sugar and grated nutmeg to taste.

Mode: Beat the egg, mixing with it a tablespoonful of cold water; make the wine and the rest of the water hot, but not boiling: pour it on the egg, stirring all the time. Add sufficient lump sugar to sweeten the mixture, and a little grated nutmeg; put all into a very clean saucepan, set it on a gentle fire, and stir the contents one way until they thicken, but *do not allow them to boil.* Serve in a glass with snippets of toasted bread or plain crisp biscuits. When the egg is not warmed, the mixture will be found easier of digestion, but it is not so pleasant a drink.

Sufficient for 1 person.

CLARET CUP

Ingredients: 1 bottle of claret, 1 pint bottle of champagne, 1 bottle of seltzer or soda, 1 glass of maraschino, 2 peaches or a few slices of pineapple, 3 or 4 tablespoonfuls of powdered sugar, borage.

Mode: Put the sugar in a jug and pour over the claret and liqueur, and stand in ice. When wanted, put the peaches sliced, or the pineapple, into a bowl, then pour over the contents of the jug, the champagne and the seltzer, both of which may be iced, put in the borage and let it stand for a few minutes before serving.

Average cost, 5s.

Sufficient for 6 persons.

A CAPITAL 'NIGHTCAP'

Ingredients: 4 lumps of sugar, 4 drops of essence of cloves, $\frac{1}{2}$ pint of strong ale, 1 wineglassful of brandy.

Mode: Drop the essence on the sugar, put all the ingredients into a saucepan, and drink the mixture hot, just before bedtime.

Average Cost, 6d.

Good Morning

'Heaviness may endure for a night,
but joy cometh in the morning.'

Whatever the horrors of the night, day always comes. Do you not know that delicious dreamy feeling when one first wakes on a summer morning, with the twitter of birds in the air, and the fresh breeze coming in at the open window – when, lying lazily with eyes half shut, one sees as in a dream green boughs waving, or waters rippling in a golden light? It is a pleasure very near to sadness, bringing tears to one's eyes like a beautiful picture or poem. And if you are a child is not that a Mother's sweet voice that summons you to rise? To rise and forget, in the bright sunlight, the ugly dreams that frightened you so when all was dark – to rise and enjoy another happy day, first kneeling to thank that unseen Friend, who sends you the beautiful sun?

A nightcap of a different sort: what the well-dressed clergyman wears to bed.

Calming Calculations

1 Place 8 pigs in the first sty, 10 in the second, nothing in the third, and 6 in the fourth: 10 is nearer ten than 8; nothing is nearer ten than 10; 6 is nearer ten than nothing; and 8 is nearer ten than 6.

2 Ten. Adding the wounds together, we get $70 + 75 + 80 + 85 = 310$, among 100 men; which gives 3 to each, and 4 to 10 men. Therefore the least percentage is 10.

3 In $6\frac{1}{4}$ minutes.

4 Ten.

5 In Shylock's bargain for the flesh was found
    No mention of the blood that flowed around:
So when the stick was sawed in eight,
    The sawdust lost diminished from the weight.

6 As curly-headed Jemmy was sleeping in bed,
His brother John gave him a blow on the head;
James opened his eyelids, and spying his brother,
Doubled his fist, and gave him another.
This kind of box then is not so rare;
The lids are the eyelids, the locks are the hair,
And so every schoolboy can tell to his cost,
The key to the tangles is constantly lost.

7 'Twixt 'Perhaps' and 'May be'
    Little difference we see:
Let the question go round,
    The answer is found.

8 That salmon and sole Puss should think very grand
    Is no such remarkable thing.
For more of these dainties Puss took up her stand;
But when the third sister stretched out her fair hand
    Pray why should Puss swallow her ring?

9 'In these degenerate days', we oft hear said,
    'Manners are lost and chivalry is dead!'
  No wonder, since in high exalted spheres
    The same degeneracy, in fact, appears.
  The Moon, in social matters interfering,
    Scolded the Sun, when early in appearing:
  And the rude Sun, her gentle sex ignoring,
    Called her a fool, thus her pretensions flooring.

10 Five seeing, and seven blind
    Give us twelve, in all, we find;
  But all of these, 'tis very plain,
    Come into account again.
  For take notice, it may be true,
    That those blind of one eye are blind for two;
  And consider contrariwise,
    That to see with your eye you may have your eyes:
  So setting one against the other—
    For a mathematician no great bother—
  And working the sum, you will understand
    That sixteen wise men still trouble the land.

Word Ways

1 Yvan. Rab is 'bar' reversed. Ymra is 'army' reversed.
2 Magpie.
3 Lemon.
4 The phrase is an anagram of 'Florence Nightingale'.
5 The phrase is an anagram of 'William Ewart Gladstone'.

Tangrams

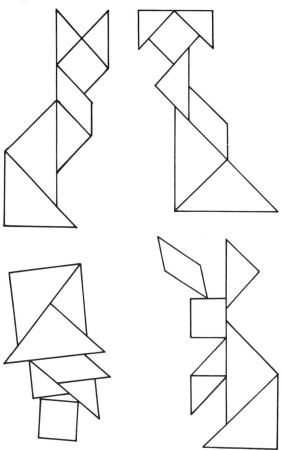

Charade

I-MAGI-NATION

Doublets

1 EEL	2 POOR	3 RAVEN	4 OAT	5 TREE
een	boor	riven	rat	free
pen	book	risen	rot	flee
pin	rook	riser	roe	fled
PIE	rock	MISER	RYE	feed
	rick			weed
	RICH			weld
				wold
				WOOD

6 GRASS	7 APE	8 CAIN	9 FLOUR	10 TEA
crass	are	chin	floor	sea
cress	ere	shin	flood	set
tress	err	spin	blood	sot
trees	ear	spun	brood	HOT
frees	mar	spud	broad	
freed	MAN	sped	BREAD	
greed		aped		
GREEN		abed		
		ABEL		

11 COMB	12 ROGUE	13 ELM	14 ARMY	15 BEANS
come	vogue	ell	arms	beams
home	vague	all	aims	seams
hole	value	ail	dims	shams
hale	valve	air	dams	shame
hall	halve	fir	dame	shale
hail	heave	far	name	shall
HAIR	helve	oar	nave	shell
	leave	OAK	NAVY	SHELF
	lease			
	least			
	BEAST			

16 HOOK	17 QUELL	18 FURIES	19 BUY	20 MINE
hoot	quill	buries	bud	mint
host	quilt	buried	bid	mist
hist	guilt	burked	aid	most
fist	guile	barked	aim	moat
FISH	guide	barred	arm	coat
	glide	BARREL	ark	COAL
	glade		ask	
	grade		ASS	
	grave			
	brave			
	BRAVO			

21 COSTS	22 ONE	23 BLUE	24 BLACK	25 FISH
posts	owe	glue	blank	fist
pests	ewe	glut	blink	gist
tests	eye	gout	clink	girt
tents	dye	pout	chink	gird
tenth	doe	port	chine	BIRD
tench	toe	part	whine	
teach	too	pant	WHITE	
peach	TWO	pint		
peace		PINK		
PENCE				